The Magic of Banking – The Coming Collapse

by

Godfrey Bloom
TD RCDS(s)

Grosvenor House
Publishing Limited

The right of Godfrey Bloom to be identified as the author of this
work has been asserted in accordance with Section 78
of the Copyright, Designs and Patents Act 1988

The book cover picture is copyright to Godfrey Bloom

This book is published by
Grosvenor House Publishing Ltd
Link House
140 The Broadway, Tolworth, Surrey, KT6 7HT.
www.grosvenorhousepublishing.co.uk

A CIP record for this book
is available from the British Library

ISBN 978-1-78148-996-3

FOREWORD

The world stands on the edge of the abyss. A financial crisis of its own making. How did it come about? Where did it all go wrong? What can be done to salvage the coming collapse of banking and fiat currencies across the world?

Banking and monetary disasters are not new. Historically, such fiascos have been limited to very few major countries at any one time, the most well-known and textbook case was the Weimar Republic. Of particular importance because Germany is a major economic power. Minor banking and currency collapses are simply part of world history.

They have been so frequent that there is a strong collectors market in government bonds, the actual paper. Works of art in their own right. In fact, the more ornate the bond script and artwork usually the more unreliable the issue (mostly a thing of the past however as the modern world is now driven by electronic currencies).

What is so different today from the crises of yesteryear? The new phenomenon is worldwide. In the past, there has always been a fall-back position. In the nineteenth century, sterling was the reserve currency of the world, while in the twentieth century it is the US dollar. Still the case today, but hanging on by its metaphorical fingernails.

In 2008, the first terrible rumblings of the looming financial crisis were felt. The banks were broke and the world knew it.

"Fiat currencies can collapse in just weeks"

German Paper Marks per U.S. Dollar 1922 to 1923
Logarithmic Scale (Base 10) Monthly Average (Federal Reserve Board)

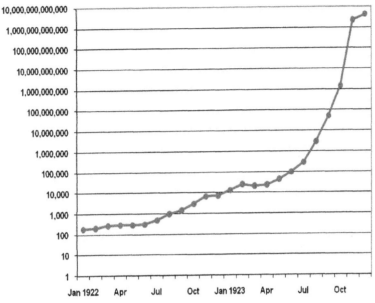

Source: http://www.shadowstats.com/article/hyperinflation-2010

As banks are built on faith and confidence when that ephemeral foundation crumbles, so too does the system. Central bankers are the last resort lenders; this is not just a glib academic phrase; it is the central bankers raison-d'etre. These central banks have no money of their own but can create money with political support.

In days gone by they would turn the printing presses, actually manufacture notes and transfer them to anywhere the fiscal hole needed to be plugged. Today they are typed into a computer and money is created out of thin air. The technical term is quantitative easing. More vulgarly money printing, perhaps more accurately: counterfeiting. This would be the term used if it were carried out by anyone but a central bank. Political support means taxpayer underwritten.

Give anyone a machine that can print money and they will use it. Not with any malfeasance in mind, usually by governments with a view to the common good. But, there is always a political dynamic, always an election pending, always a mini crisis that needs addressing, always a special case. The State can only cope with its extraordinary self-imposed responsibilities with money. As governments extend their remit, they expand their requirement for it. They can tax or borrow, but they are not immune from market forces with these two facilities. Too much tax creates a fiscal drag on economic growth, as does borrowing. In this, governments face the same restrictions as a business or indeed the common man. The recourse therefore is to money printing.

This printing takes the form of bond issuance in short debt. Again government is not immune from the responsibility of debt servicing, a coupon must be paid. So, even more fiscal drag, just another term for stifled economic growth.

This aide memoire is designed to help the interested, educated layman to understand the problem rather solve it.

Without an understanding of how it came about no solution can be found.

It is very clear now the 2008 crisis was not understood, this means none of the problems have gone away, indeed they remain but are much worse today than they were then.

1. WHAT IS MONEY?

Money is not taught in schools, a rather gaping hole in a young person's education. There are many books on the subject, but for those without the time or the inclination, this aide-memoire will just outline the basics. For only the basics are necessary to understand the forthcoming crisis.

Money is simply a medium of exchange; it is not wealth in its own right. Historically, money has taken many forms, usually something with intrinsic value in its own right, something difficult to counterfeit which would devalue the medium. Gold and silver have fulfilled this role for thousands of years but special circumstances often make local money more practical. North America in the 18th century traded

"Never mistake paper for gold"

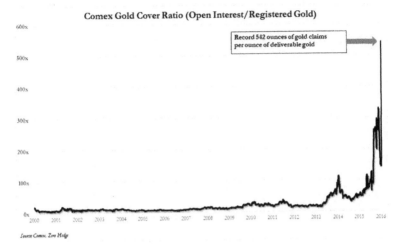

Comex Gold Cover Ratio (Open Interest/Registered Gold)

Record 542 ounces of gold claims per ounce of deliverable gold

Source: Comex, Zero Hedge

Source: Zero Hedge: http://www.zerohedge.com/news/2016-03-04/
blackrock-supsends-gold-etf-issuance-due-demand-gold

beaver pelts, Berlin in 1945 due to a shortage of reserve fiat currencies promoted the use of cigarettes, nylons and whiskey. The medium in itself is not important; the requirement only is that it is broadly accepted as a store of value.

Without money trade would be reduced to barter, a desperately inefficient system precluding a division of labour and its benefits to the living standards of mankind.

But money is a sensitive plant totally dependent on trust, hence the long term preference for gold and silver which is an internationally recognized medium with a value with London to Bombay to Shanghai and on to New York. It is also a long term store of wealth. Gold salvaged from shipwrecks today carries the same value as yesteryear. A British gold sovereign will buy this week what it bought one hundred years ago. This is why it is still a popular store of wealth particularly in the East.

So how does this square with fiat (or paper currency)? Lugging heavy gold about soon became impractical for both national and international trade. Banking therefore stepped in

to facilitate trade by promissory notes. The bank kept the gold safe and issued a piece of paper in the form of a bank note such as we see today. Older readers will remember the wording on the Bank of England five-pound note, 'I promise to pay the bearer on demand the sum in gold'. Each note was backed by gold, indeed if it were not, no one would have accepted it.

Mankind though has a great flaw: his love of war. Wars have to be paid for, they are expensive. Since Roman times, all sorts of shenanigans went on with coin clipping or alloy reduction of gold content to meet the cost. In more modern times countries took their currencies off the gold standard, they just issued paper. This worked in the short term but degraded the currency in the long term with inflation. A dollar bill in the early 1970s when America was on the gold standard is now worth in purchasing power about eight cents.

European countries are no different.

The euros, dollars or pounds in your pocket are intrinsically worthless. Only a common acceptance of it gives it value.

"Without gold backing a dollar bill is just paper"

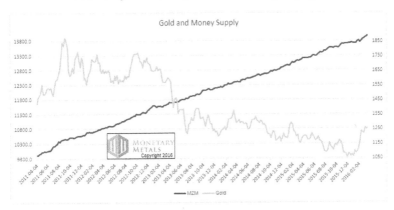

Source: Monetary Metals: https://monetary-metals.com/the-gold-money-supply-correlation-report-3-apr-2016/

"You will notice the Russians are not stupid, they buy bullion not paper"

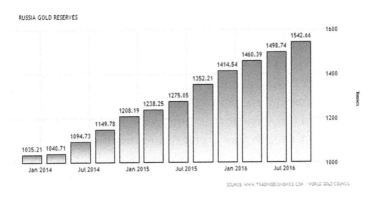

Source: www.tradingeconomics.com

This can be perfectly ephemeral; history is littered with failed currencies. There is a general perception in the west that major countries cannot go bankrupt, currencies will not fail, those fundamental economic laws which apply to you and your family do not apply to the state. We examine this dangerous illusion in the next chapter.

2. HOW DO BANKS OPERATE?

Banks fulfil a number of roles, basically, they grease the wheels of commerce. Money is a store of value and banks offer an international settlement. Deposit your money in Barclays in London and you can settle accounts for goods ordered in Hong Kong. These days it is all electronically done in a few seconds. Assuming all parties have confidence in the system it works very well. Banking is the counterparty to money, it depends on trust. This trust can disappear on the slightest suspicion that a bank is not solvent. It leads to what is known as a 'run on the bank'. This is a periodic occurrence across the globe, has been and ever will be. The system is desperately fragile. Why?

Retail banks have to do the impossible. The financial equivalent of defying gravity. They borrow short but lend long. An example: a businessman or old age pensioner, deposits say £100,000. The bank lends it to your son or daughter for a house, the repayment period is 25 years, it charges interest to the borrower and pays interest to the depositor and keeps a margin for the bank. All of this you know, but that is only part of the story. The system is slightly more complex. The depositor imagines his or her money remains theirs in the same way a farmer stores his grain with a corn merchant. But this is not so. The deposit becomes the property of the bank. Moreover, the bank is only required by regulation to keep 10% reserves.

So the £100,000 deposit becomes but £10,000, the remainder having been lent on. Let us imagine for a moment that £90,000 is then sent to another bank, which is in turn only required to keep 10%, it holds £9,000 and lends the balance.

We are assuming here for ease of explanation that the international Basel III banking regulation demands this reserve. Let us also make the not unreasonable assumption that some of these bank loans go wrong. Perhaps because times are hard, a recession or some other economic shock where people are more likely to want their bank deposits back to tide them over. No wild stretch of the imagination is needed to see how easily a bank can become insolvent or indeed bankrupt.

This is a well-known phenomenon but particularly bad in the crisis of 2008 when banks were heavily involved in subprime debt. Counterparty investment houses imagined they were buying safe mortgage loans to the professional middle classes on premium properties, when much of the subordinated debt was nothing of the kind. When confidence collapsed so did the banks.

"How can this continue?"

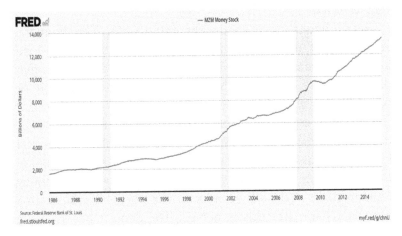

Source: Federal Bank Reserve of St Louis

What happens next? Where does the central bank come in? What is its purpose?

It seems as if central banks have been with us forever, not so. They are a relatively recent idea. The famous US Fed is a child of 1913, the Bank of England was not nationalised until after WWII. Don't let anyone tell you central banks are

"Britain is awash with fake money which is why
your children can't afford a house"

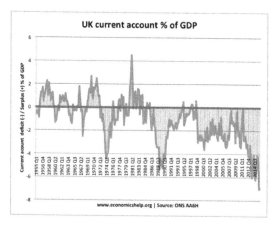

independent; the governors are all political appointees. In the
end, he who pays the piper calls the tune, it was ever thus.

By controlling the money supply, either by contraction or
expansion they control interest rates and remain the lender of
last resort. They can print money and rescue failed retail
banks with taxpayers money and they do. The last dramatic
rescue by the BoE (Bank of England) was in 2008, the Fed
likewise.

These bailouts cost the public sums of money beyond
human imagination. They were simply put on the national
debt. Trillions of dollars, pounds and euros just put on
account for future generations to somehow pay off. Such is
the enormity of the debts and the cost of servicing them
that it is conceivable they can be repaid. It is impossible to
illustrate the extent of this debt to an electorate which quite
naturally struggles with numbers above a few hundred
million.

UK national debt is growing at an estimated £5,000 per
second. The Institute for Economic Affairs has made the best
attempt at explaining the inexplicable. Their website is worth
a look.

Why have banks and governments got into such debt? Are governments somehow different from businesses or ordinary citizens? Of course not, if you continually spend more than you earn, bankruptcy follows as sure as night follows day.

The trouble is western democracies are in the grip of a failed economic theory. It is generally known as Keynesianism. This is not an A level economics prima, but suffice to say the theory suggests in times of recession, crisis or threatened depression, state spending can rescue an economy. For eighty years this hypothesis has held sway. It has never worked anywhere in the world but it is the only school of economics taught in state universities in Europe or America, so it has become holy writ. It remains totally unchallenged in politics or media.

But debt, public spending, and money printing cannot last forever. Even the International Monetary Fund and European Central Bank have now counselled caution. Without serious reform, the outlook must deteriorate, perhaps much quicker than anyone anticipated.

So far only public debt has been considered, private debt is at an all-time high across the globe. Derivatives, which are not strictly speaking debt are still a liability.

3. YIELDS AND INTEREST

A word or two on yield or interest. In the past the market governed interest rates. The price of money if you prefer. What is the point of interest? Where does it fit into the scheme of things?

Spending money is about time preference. Shall I buy a product today or wait a bit? If I wait and save more I can afford a better product, or you might want to just defer all big purchases until later. Perhaps to build protection against an unforeseen circumstance, or retirement or the possible arrival of children. The options are limitless. This is simply time preference.

However if there is no reward for thrift in the shape of compensation, interest, it destabilises the concept of time preference. If you can buy that product today by borrowing at very low interest it seems tempting, it revs up the economy does it not? After all received wisdom is economies are driven by 'aggregate demand', a popular academic misunderstanding of how economies really work. If you think about it how on earth could wealth be created by consumption?

A bit counter intuitive is it not? Your next door neighbour's son buys a two year old Mercedes sports car, very nice too, but he has borrowed the money. His time preference decision has been made. Not an unreasonable one at that. The neighbour gets his car, the salesman makes his commission, but the money has been created electronically. In the old days the lad would have saved his money accruing interest and bought the car in three years time. He would have earned real money which would have been invested into the economy, it would have worked to create wealth.

But with zero interest fewer people are inclined to invest, there is no motivation to do so. So the world lives on artificial fake money for consumption today. But let us look at other aspects of the economy outside the fool's gold of aggregate demand. As mentioned earlier bonds have their yields reduced dramatically, does this matter? Not to the young man next door, he has his car, even if he cannot afford to keep up the payments the worst they can do is repossess the car. No big deal. Or is it?

If there is a recession millions of young men across the globe default on their loans. Millions of now ageing Mercedes & BMWs are dumped on the market, the assets are significantly less than the loan book. The monetised debt bought by amongst others the ECB becomes junk rated, any of this familiar?

Because the money supply is grossly inflated real estate, bonds and stocks become overpriced. The money might not have inflated the CPI but it has sent assets through the roof.

Yet savers & pensioners rely on yield, of which there is now none. Pension funds are destroyed, savings are worthless old people suffer. Without yield pensioners in retirement suffer no discretionary increases, life assurance companies struggle, endowments and whole life plans are subject to drastic underfunding, so are all other classes of insurance, no yield means no reserve, premiums soar. But what of the young man with his lovely car? And all those other young people with their fancy cars or holidays? It is not good news at all really because they cannot afford their first house, so they live with their parents or pay monster rent.

Who therefore is getting a result from this lunatic asylum system of money and banking?

Only politicians and bankers, the debt is inflated away over time, in thirty years no one can understand why a pint of beer is £25, why houses are out of the reach of even middle aged professional people in the big cities. Why their pension payments are derisory. Why the national debt is a number beyond human comprehension why does the economy not grow, why have middle class living standards stagnated for an entire generation?

The answer is neither the media, press, bankers, academics, politicians or the electorate understood money and banking.

4. WHAT'S NEW?

So far everything you have read could have come out of any State University textbook. Now it starts to get more interesting. Banking and finance move at a rapid pace. As an academic discipline economics moves much faster than others. It is a living beast. History, mathematics, geography, even physics move at a snail's pace in comparison.

What might have been true thirty years ago is no longer relevant. Look at computers, cars and telephones of thirty years ago, unrecognisable today. Why would banking be different? Yet, in the State classrooms, textbooks and recommended reading have barely changed.

Money is now created in a much broader way than years ago. Commercial banks create most of the money in circulation, how so?

If you go into your bank today and fill out a successful application for a loan your bank will facilitate a deposit account allowing you to draw upon it. Let us assume it was for a car, you buy your car for the twenty thousand pounds agreed, the seller deposits the money in his bank, bingo your bank has an asset in its loan book, the seller's bank has a deposit. Suddenly there are forty thousand pounds in the banking system where until yesterday there was none. This goes on every day all over the world. The technical term for this is credit boom.

If you look at banking regulation (let's keep it simple), a bank's loan book is shown as an asset on an agreed regulatory sliding scale. 100% of the purchase of sovereign debt, down to just 20% for a loan to a small business. No surprise that banks prefer to make their profit at the bottom end of the risk scale.

This is why anecdotally you will find small businesses complaining about the uncooperative nature of their bank when they want to expand but the housing market is awash with cash fuelling out of control real estate prices.

"The inevitable result of going off gold and giving politicians a money machine"

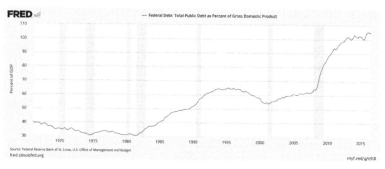

Source: https://fred.stlouisfed.org/series/GFDEGDQ188S#0

Where is the danger for banks? The same as it was in 2008. Nothing has changed except the numbers which are now bigger than ever. Consider those 'assets', the regulatory system (Basel III) encourages. Sovereign debt, most of which is really junk status, Italian, French and Irish bonds. Monetised packaged debt, everything from your neighbour's mortgage to your son's second-hand car loan.

If we accept a broad requirement of a ten percent reserve ratio for banks it is not difficult to see that a cyclical recession only needs a modest fall in any of these assets to break most commercial banks. Indeed, a close look at their assets would probably expose such a fall even now, particularly the banks of the Mediterranean basin.

Public and private debt across the globe stands at such a number there would be no room in this aide memoire to print in full, just too many noughts. Moreover, it would be meaningless, the sort of number usually associated with space travel at the edge of the Galaxy.

Most individuals incur debt for a specific reason, the purchase of houses and goods. The loans have a finite lifespan, say three years for a car to twenty-five for a house.

The government has no such constraint. They borrow to pay off previous loans, they create money by issuing bonds, the debt spirals daily. Yet, as there is no restraint there can be no end game for the banking/political dynamic except an Armageddon of hitherto unprecedented scale. In the next chapter we will look in more detail at the mechanics of money creation by the State.

So far we can deduce perhaps just one thing for sure, that money in a modern society is created by modern day witchcraft.

It is so complex most academic economists don't understand it – as one glance at university textbooks demonstrates. Few bankers understand it and no politicians either. If all these people who make up the great and the good of the financial world did, the system would not collapse with such monotonous

regularity. In 2008 it was the shadow banking system that dragged western banks in the quagmire. But mark this for irony; there is no accepted definition of the term 'shadow banking'. So ephemeral is the concept we are not even clear what it is. What we do know is it dominates international banking and remains off balance sheet, being off balance sheet are unregulated. Not that financial regulation has much of a track record. We understand from the Austrian School of Economics regulation is all but impossible without perfect knowledge of a market. This in itself is absurdly impossible. Modern derivatives of which most shadow bank assets consist are little more than a nod and a wink between bankers. Bear in mind most lending is inter-bank rather than directly to private borrowers. Given that most individual and commercial organizations use banks the money stays in the system.

The German banks are believed to be owed £900 billion by the shadow banking system. Largely from European banks which are fundamentally insolvent. The ECB is attempting to keep this unsustainable financial merry go round alive by buying £80 billion of commercial and sovereign bonds every

month. Some of these bonds are more worthless than others, but most are if not junk status grossly overpriced. Would you lend money to a government for 2% per annum for 20 years when that country already had debt liabilities of £5 trillion and inflation at 1.5%? That incidentally is what a UK government gilt asks you to do. As a point of academic interest 338% of GDP!

The Maastricht Treaty envisaged these sorts of financial political shenanigans and forbade the purchase of bonds

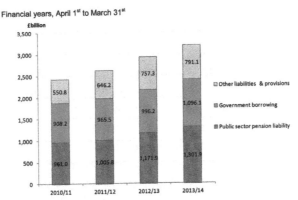

"Just imagine if this was your family's position"

Financial years, April 1st to March 31st

£billion

http://www.ons.gov.uk/ons/guide-method/method-quality/specific/economy/
public-sector-finances/public-sector-finances---wider-measures-of-public-
sector-net-debt.pdf

directly under article 101 of the treaty. But finance and political expediency will always find a way, the ECB now buys them on the secondary market.

Bond yields are now so low and bank deposits interest is entering negative territory, crucifying pension funds and savings. Harming pensioners at one end of the social scale and producing mass youth unemployment at the other.

"Observe the widening gap in pension deficit funding. Notice particularly when it started. Nothing to do with BREXIT"

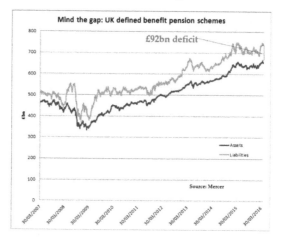

Source: http://www.independent.co.uk/news/business/news/the-chart-that-shows-how-big-the-pensions-deficit-at-uk-firms-has-grown-a7015256.html

Many make the mistake of blaming the euro for the demise of many of the EU economies. This is to misunderstand the role of money. Austrian School economists endorse 'hard money', that which has been traditionally backed by gold or silver. An historical exception being the ancient Sumerian use of tally sticks, inherently valueless but effective for hundreds of years.

The hard money theorists of today argue that fiat currency will always inevitably produce periodic banking crises. This, however, is the result of human behavior so expertly expounded by Von Mises. This is true today, economic depressions are not caused by the euro any more than people are killed by guns.

The problem is the human element. The single currency requires fiscal responsibility; the mores of the euro are the result of western social and corporate welfare and universal suffrage. In short, anyone who has a machine that can print money will do so. Especially politicians to whom the next election result is the goal, not the long-term success of the economy. The euro is but the symptom of the monetary disease, not the cause.

The modern banking system is irrevocably flawed. It does not protect the vulnerable, it does not facilitate small business which is the lifeblood of any economy and it rewards one class of the community over another, debtors over savers. Although the State pretends inflation is subdued this is only using a government formula, CPI that much manipulated index only reflects part of the picture. Asset price inflation is rampant as anyone with grown-up children trying to buy a house understands only too well.

Moreover, it builds a debt too great for the human mind to conceive. The end game must come and come perhaps sooner than we think.

5. WHAT'S THE DEBATE?

The financial crisis of 2008 triggered interest rate reductions on an unprecedented scale. The Bank of England rate fell from 5% to the current 0.5%. In the Eurozone, rates fell from 4.25% to 0%. The BoE balance sheet soared from 22% growth in January 2008 to 163.8% in October of the same year. The ECB accelerated its growth from 15.3% in January 2008 to 55% the following November.

What does this mean though to you and your family?

A credit explosion inflates the money supply. It finds its way piecemeal into the economy; those who benefit most are those on the initial receiving end, the technical term for this is the Cantillon effect. Simply put those with assets benefit as

"Note again the timings of heavy stress on pension funding.
Directly commensurate with QE and massive interest cuts"

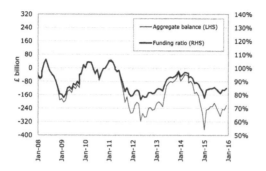

Source: http://www.pensionprotectionfund.org.uk/DocumentLibrary/
Documents/PPF_7800_January_16.pdf

prices rise. For those with none, the prospect of ever owning any recedes yet further.

This is most apparent in house prices, but more importantly and not so obvious to the layman, inflated bond prices. This manifests itself in historically low yields. This has the knock on effect of making your pension fund insolvent. The public sector is protected because the taxpayer covers the position. It is also disastrous for savers, many of whom are old age pensioners. Low-interest rates benefit debtors over creditors, a disastrous form of social financial engineering. The search for yield forces investors into heavier risk assets, overvalued stock markets and poor quality monetised loans. The very thing that triggered the 2008 meltdown in the first place.

In an earlier chapter, we saw just how fragile the capital adequacy of banks was international. A correction of only 10% of reserve assets forces a bank into insolvency. Hardly an unimaginable or even unprecedented phenomenon. Notice the careful word 'correction'. Not a crash, a relatively modest fall can break the banks. The US Fed and Bank of Japan are all in the same position.

This credit binge, both public and private is worldwide, it is being sustained by more and more credit. No one knows how to jump from the runaway train, we can't get off but we can't stay on.

The whole fiat currency and banking system is based on faith, confidence if you prefer. The first bank to break will bring down all the others, interbank lending will collapse as it did in 2008 only on a scale now eight times worse. Banks will no longer be too big to fail but too big to rescue.

At present politicians, press, media, bankers and civil servants are in denial. There is no informed debate. The situation in China is beyond western understanding.

Just to give an understandable number the national debt in Great Britain is £80,000 for every family in the land, that is a modest estimate.

In 2008 her Majesty Queen Elizabeth asked why no one saw the disaster coming? When the inevitable crash comes on an awesome scale she will ask the same question again.

6. CURRENCY EXPLAINED

There always appears to be some confusion when I talk to university undergraduates on the underlying nuances of central bankers. This is indeed a dark art. Hedge fund managers used to play back Alan Greenspan interviews in slow time to see which eyebrows twitched. Did he mean what he said or was it just rhetoric? I have eyeballed two ECB Presidents, Jean Trichet and Mario Draghi. You have to be really close, you must understand body language, eye contact, phraseology as I say a dark art. One thing you cannot do is read a transcript. It would be like playing poker in a blindfold. Yet journalists often do.

You also have to know what to ask a central banker, my website gives an example of this when I bullied Draghi into an indiscretion, it's on my website for those interested although a few years old.

Politics doesn't really move currency markets short of armed confrontation. Or a change of government with diametrically opposed fiscal policy. This is now very rare, as all western democracies are broadly Keynesian. In short print money, spend, borrow, fiscal rectitude is a thing of the past. Don't trust the rhetoric look at the numbers. This is a field where numbers are king.

Greenspan, Bernanke, Janet Yellen at the Fed are fairly inscrutable. You never know if they will raise interest rates or not. They never do because it is impossible, in the hearts of traders and investors they know this but they always leave a tiny space for doubt. Being a central banker is a bit like being an army officer. At Sandhurst we were told 'never bleed in front of the men'. Central Banking is about confidence, nothing else, without it the system collapses.

Even a slight inkling that all is not well will depress currencies. Sometimes that is what bankers intend, a word here, a shrug there to take a rising currency off the boil. Who could forget Greenspan's 'irrational exuberance'? Delicious innuendo designed to take the heat out of the stock market.

QE or money printing if you prefer will automatically depress a currency, even only in the short term. The implication it is a permanent feature will tank the currency and a further suggestion interest rates will remain on zero will depress it further. Overt concern over the banks economy will likewise murder the currency. When a central banker confirms permanent QE, low interest rates 'because he or she fears a rocky patch ahead' you have a fire sale.

This is now as we all know what Mark Carney at the BoE has done. It is inconceivable that this could have been an accident. Moreover central bankers are political appointees so this must be agreed at a very senior level. If there is an added complication such as a national debt beyond human comprehension crashing the currency takes debt off the bottom line. Sadly for ordinary working folk the baby goes straight out with the bath water.

Who gets it in the neck? Savers, pensioners, importers of goods & raw materials. Shouldn't this be illegal? Well, it was in the Middle Ages, degraders of coin of the realm had their hands and feet cut off. Should we reinstate that barbaric punishment?

Certainly not, a simple hanging is quite sufficient.

7. THE MYTH OF
A COMPETITIVE CURRENCY

One of the great currency myths is devaluation somehow benefits an economy. Not too much of course, just a bit. This is rather a subjective judgement, what should the value of sterling be against the dollar? The Euro? The Yen? After all, they are all fundamentally worthless. Why would their value vary? We know banks create money electronically in a rather random way, we also know a country's central bank (for central bank read taxpayer) attempt to second guess world markets to favour certain sections of their electorate.

Exports as a percentage of GDP vary from country to country, they are incidentally a terrible formula for judging a nations well-being but let us leave that for a moment and take

"Debasement of the Pound"

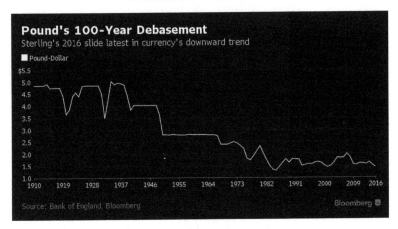

Pound's 100-Year Debasement
Sterling's 2016 slide latest in currency's downward trend

■ Pound-Dollar

Source: Bank of England, Bloomberg

the numbers at face value. In the United States, the figure is reckoned to be about ten percent, the UK 12%, Germany much more, it matters not, it is history that matters, empirical evidence not economic dogma.

Your economy has much less to do with companies exporting goods or services abroad than government's lead you to believe. It is possible you live in a town with a dominant

"Note the significant strengthening of the Deutsche Mark and the Yen, but both countries dominate in the field of exports. Thus blowing the myth of a 'competitive currency helping an economy.' It is indeed counter intuitive, but look at the numbers"

Real Effective Exchange Rates, 1975 - 89

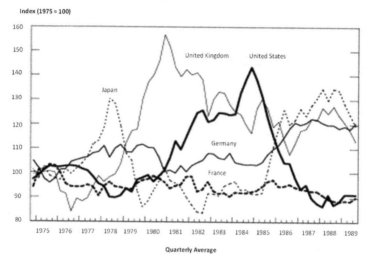

Source: http://www.imf.org/external/pubs/ft/silent/

export industry. Nissan in Sunderland for example or Honda in Leicetershire but most of us don't. Your economy is micro; indeed, all economies are micro. Macro is a concept invented by academic economists who delight in theory but have very little understanding of the realities of their subject. Which is why they are nearly always wrong. Look around you , your economy is the cab driver, shop keeper, hairdresser, doctor, teacher, electrician, dentist, decorator, gardener and all the other small businesses and individuals. Do they benefit from an artificially depressed currency? The perceived economic wisdom is that they do, but think through, how can they?

The UK is a massive importer of manufactured goods and raw materials. All of which has to be paid in foreign currencies.

The tyres you put on your car, the petrol you put in it, the radio you switch on to listen to the news as you drive to work. The same when you renew your mobile phone or TV. You go on holiday to get some sunshine, your food, drink and accommodation have to be paid in foreign currencies. Almost everything you do or buy has become more expensive. Of course, some people benefit, an export company gains a measure of advantage but it is ephemeral, their workforce wants higher wages to compensate for inflation, raw material costs are higher, benefits are modest. It is worth looking at post-war Germany.

Under the bold and brilliant leadership of Ludwig Erhard (a man with a great vision), he embraced laissez-faire capitalism in the teeth of hostile opposition from every quarter, the result was soaring exports in manufactured goods for three decades and rising living standards which are the wonder of historians today. Whilst Great Britain wallowed in centralized planning, archaic socialism and welfarism. Yet the German mark was gradually increasing in value against all other global currencies. Proving it is not currencies that need

to be made 'competitive' but production. German cars are not world renowned because they are cheap but because they offer value for money.

Politicians and their cronies in the banks devalue currencies, not for the benefit of working people but to inflate their debt away, helping themselves to share when it still has value.

Politicians and central bankers you will note enjoy inflation proofed pensions and salaries, an option not available to most of us.

Just pause for a moment, would you sooner own today a 1908 pound note or a gold sovereign? A one-hundred-year-old dollar bill or its equivalent in gold?

The next time anyone suggests devalue the currency is good, have a look at his pension plan.

8. SUMMARY

The previous chapters have been devoted to how the system works, it has hopefully been informative and not too judgemental. But this aide memoire does beg a number of questions, how do we get out of this terrible not so merry-go-round of ever increasing public and private debt? Clearly it is impossible, the debt is of a scale far beyond rescue.

Private debt must find its own way but public debt needs to be at least curtailed, there is no evidence anywhere in the democratic world that there is the political will to do so, indeed it is probably impossible to get elected in a modern democracy where clients of the state both corporate and social have a vested interest in the status quo. Land owners on their estates are as protective of their subsidies as the permanently unemployed on their rather less salubrious estates. The only people to gain from reform are the wealth creating sector of middle England.

The butcher, baker, hairdresser, cab driver & mechanic.

All those people living lives of quiet desperation trying to make ends meet in the teeth of ever increasing rules, regulation and tax. There are just too few of them left in an economy struggling under the weight of a civil service burden unprecedented in British history.

Only electoral reform can save modern economies from ultimate bankruptcy, this will not happen.

Step back a moment if you will, forget jargon, forget the great and the good explaining black is white to bewildered TV and radio presenters and ponder this.

We have a political system which enfranchises every citizen over the tender age of eighteen.

It is the sole criterion. Nothing could be further from the original concept of democracy in Ancient Greece where contribution to society was a prerequisite. As Oliver Cromwell said a man must do more than breath the air to be entitled to a vote. Moreover with the exception of Switzerland modern democracies have representative systems. The party system if you will, or closer to the truth government by lobby. The concept is, as it must always be corrupt.

This political machinery owns the monetary system, it controls the banks, it controls legal tender laws.

Whatever the State does, no matter how supposedly pro bono publico its ideals money remains simply a medium of exchange, interest rates reflect time preference and individual circumstance. No public policy can make currency become anything else any more than legislation can make water flow up hill.

The end game is now playing out. The extraordinary thing is when the collapse comes history shows us people will not blame government but believe there was not enough government. They will turn to the same people who created the disaster to extract them from it.

Should you doubt this common sense ask yourself this question. Is my family or business not subject to the laws of financial gravity? Can I spend continuously more money than I earn every year without going broke? Is there some magic formula that means my country can do things I cannot?

Is the chancellor not subject to the same basic rules as my family?

APPENDIX A: DON'T BLAME THE EURO

What is a 'common currency'?

It is most irritating to hear Eurosceptics argue that the common currency is the source of Europe's woes, there are indeed many sources but the euro is not one of them. I have already written a previous article going into some detail on the subject of money, I do not intend to cover old ground but just to remind readers money is simply a medium of exchange which allows the fruitful division of labour and the avoidance of barter in trade. It is nothing else, just a convenience in the modern world. There has been a common currency since the advent of world economies. Research shows it has ranged historically from salt to beaver pelts, nylons to cigarettes, but for thousands of years globally it has usually been gold or silver coin.

We know gold coinage has been debased by and by adding alloys or trimming, nothing new in that. But a common currency never the less. In Ethiopia in the nineteenth century for some unexplained reason silver Maria Theresa coins were the only acceptable currency, but leaving that aside a silver dollar or gold sovereign or any permutation would have been and still is today regarded as true money.

It is thought paper money first came into being in China in the thirteenth century but that is not important, paper was simply a promissory note to save the inconvenience or danger of carrying gold. The precious metal was redeemable in specie on production of the note. This system worked for hundreds of years, indeed it worked until the unholy alliance between bankers and politicians which we have today. This alliance together with legal tender laws have ensured paper notes can be printed without the inconvenience of providing precious metal on demand. This paper is of course inherently worthless.

How did the Euro come about?

The concept of the euro is to provide a common paper currency for all EU members, albeit with agreed restrictions, these rules were designed to protect participants in the project from inflation by overspending or currency degradation, the modern equivalent of adding alloys or trimming. The arrangement was referred to as the Growth & Stability pact. We heard a lot about it on launch but not much since. The two golden rules were no participating country could let their economies have national debt above 60% of GDP or a budget deficit of more than 3% of GDP. This was a form of fiscal policy by mutual agreement. It was not however set in stone, EU treaties are simply for the guidance of unwise men.

What went Wrong?

These rules were broken almost immediately by everyone including Germany.

Participants whose economies were and are permanently weak were granted access to cheap money overnight. Greek borrowing rates went from 12% to 5%. German exporters enjoyed a bonanza, every Greek could afford a BMW on cheap credit. In short it was party time. Fiscal prudence could be and was abandoned.

State, corporate and private debt is at an all-time high, indeed the actual numbers are beyond human imagination.

Blaming the medium of exchange for the problems these countries now have is like blaming the barman for your hangover.

If you binge yourself into a coma and wake up with a stinking head and a huge bar tab it's your fault and nobody else's.

The disaster that is the euro today is the fault of politicians and those stupid enough to elect them.

If the common currency had been gold or silver the Mediterranean countries would still be bankrupt, but they might have seen it coming earlier without the interference of the central banks with quantative easing, shadow banking, bond purchases and all the rest of the jiggery pokery beyond the understanding of both politicians and their electorate.

Can it be fixed?

The Euro can survive but not in its current form. It must be transformed into a hard currency, backed by gold or silver, or indeed any commodity that politicians cannot manufacture at will.

The State must live within its means, it must abandon tricks designed to pretend spending consistently more than income can magically continue. The market must return as the arbiter of interest rates not central banks. This would remove the need for legal tender laws, let traders settle in any form that suits them.

The destabilisation of money can never stop until politicians are completely removed from the equation and bankers are once more bound by law, this means the end of fractional reserve banking which is simply embezzlement by any other name.

APPENDIX B: GDP EXPLAINED

Gross Domestic Product (GDP) is a figment of the State's imagination.

You draw up your chair, you switch on the telly and tune in to the news. It is all very authoritative, delivered in a manner that brooks no contradiction. Fact after fact, numbers, statistics and charts. We gaze meditatively at the screen and half listen to the droning voice of the auto cutie delivering the goods. Our subliminal radar picks up on some things in which we have a specific interest. Football results, the scores are definitive Manchester United 3 Aston Villa 1, today's hottest temperature was in central London at 82%f at midday, Europe's tallest building is the Shard at 1200 feet. Pick your own example if you will. But in a minute or two you are going to have a number shot at you with all the same authority and sincerity as the others, but the number is fake. Completely bogus, a number that has been fraudulent for generations. Needless to say it is a government number, created for the sole benefit of the state. It is GDP, Gross Domestic Product. It is the figment of the state's imagination and is replicated across the world.

In order for the state to exercise its power over people it needs to know what you have and where it may be hidden. The phenomenon can be traced to the beginning of the civilised world.

There is no shortage of examples, from the Bible which tells us of the census which sent Mary and Joseph on their journey, the Domesday Book of the English Middle Ages. Despots, Kings, Emperors, warlords, politicians need to know where the wealth is before they can devise ever more fiendish ways of stealing it. Often, historically, to fund wars. GDP is no exception, conceived in its current format in 1940, earlier attempts were made in 1695 in England to find ways of funding the Anglo Dutch war. It has been fine tuned ever since to try and reflect economies as they grow and change at an ever increasing pace. Consequently the numbers are backward looking and subjective. It matters not how many government statisticians toil over the numbers inventing different ways of cornering this ephemeral figure, they are doomed like the Flying Dutchman to sail the economic seas for eternity in vain.

They are steeped in outmoded economic theory, clutching their degrees in Keynesian or monetary theory they seek the holy grail, a true, accurate and fair value of a nation's accounts.

How do they measure it? You won't believe it.

Let us muse on the absurdities of GDP measurement, where others have analysed its short comings with charts, graphs and jargon but always conclude it is a necessary evil I just outline here the nonsense of GDP for the layman.

If the state prints money, take the British government who electronically injected £350 billion into the economy in the last 6 years, it goes into the system via the banks and comes out the other side in inflation. Not CPI or RPI yet but asset price inflation, which is why your children can't afford to live in big cities, real estate inflation. Yet the huge increase in property moves the GDP number up. Those energy subsidies which pour into windmills and solar panels increase the price of electricity, yet again this ticks up GDP. The state pursues a suicidal drugs policy but the £billions squandered advances the GDP number. Crime rises so we need more prison places and more police, it goes on the ticket. Let's develop it ad absurdum. There are millions of these and fun to list. A widower marries his housekeeper, that reduces GDP, she doesn't want sex so he goes to a prostitute, that increases GDP. Who these days doesn't pay their jobbing gardener, handyman or car cleaners in cash? It doesn't register for GDP. In other words millions of those small jobs which go to making an economic community go unregistered it is sometimes referred to as the 'informal economy'. Wild guesses estimate this at an average of 15% of GDP but impossible to call. But if you think about income tax, national insurance, pensions, maternity & paternity leave, maximum working hours, employer liability insurance, the list is endless, whatever the figure it must be growing. Italy recently increased their estimate to 30% and it meant their economy notionally overtook France and Great Britain, at the stroke of a pen! What about a tasty little war? Increased spending on tanks, guns, planes & ammunition, more soldiers recruited, up goes GDP. Where is modern development in all this? Information technology such as Google, Wikipedia and social media have put at least $150 billion into the global economy in free at delivery point information, this does not find its way into the GDP machine. If St Paul's cathedral collapsed and had to be rebuilt it would increase GDP. The list of these absurdities is literally endless. Yet the quarterly report on GDP is delivered by the TV bimbo as if it were holy writ. Usually inside their own margin of error 0.8% GDP growth per quarter is crazy with an error margin of 0.25%. The children in the City and Wall St then buy or sell stock or bonds on an assessment of what the economy might do on an extrapolation of these figures over the coming year. Screamingly ludicrous. All GDP measures, and not very accurately at that, is activity. One last analogy. Imagine assessing your children's educational progress on activity, they rush about, they fill their exercise books, they stay on in the playground with their chums after school they even keep getting Saturday morning detention because they are naughty, yet this is all positive because the bench mark is energy expended not exams past.

The pathetic excuse for modern economists is they must have something, even if it's wrong. Steeped in outdated concepts, even the term macroeconomics is an anachronism, they must have something to give their political masters. It would be more honest to try astrology the numbers could not possibly be more irrelevant.

APPENDIX C: PETRO DOLLARS

Petro dollars

Most people get about their business dealing with the currency of their country or zone. Pounds, euros, yuan, yen, they know if they visit the United States it would be dollars. Everyone understands that world commodities are traded in dollars. It is the reserve currency of the world. I suspect most folk don't really think much further than that, why would they? They have to attend to their world. What can it have to do with them?

It might be worth digging a little bit deeper. How did the dollar become the world's reserve currency? What indeed does that even mean?

What is a reserve currency?

When the world traded years ago the concept of a reserve currency would have bewildered our forebears. Money was gold and silver. You either had it for settlement or you didn't. Your creditor cared not if you settled in gold sovereigns, francs or marks. Silver coin was usually equally satisfactory. The advent of paper money was simply a convenience for trade and safety. It was a promissory note. The issuer would exchange it for gold in specie on demand. Sadly wars need to be funded so government intent upon them issued paper but without the important promissory factor.

After WWII there was an international agreement that the dollar, backed in part with gold at a fixed price would be the anchor for the main global currencies. The volatility of paper currency values against gold very soon led to international arbitrage against the real price of gold and the fake participating government fixes. This was clearly doomed in the long term and it collapsed eventually in 1971 when President Nixon took the dollar off the gold standard. Too many people wanted gold too few pieces of paper. This situation will arise again when the paper gold of exchange traded funds are found to not match the bullion claimed to exist in counterparty vaults.

Where are we now?

The world agreed to exchange commodities for paper, in particular oil. The life blood of the industrial economies. The salt if you will of the pre historic world.

For forty years the oil producing countries have been selling oil for paper, the petro dollar.

The result is the oil producing countries and their industrial cousins are awash with dollars, held mainly in the form of U.S. Treasuries.

America has had the best of this bargain, they get oil and manufactured goods in exchange for fundamentally worthless paper.

Moreover it is becoming increasingly worthless.

Let's look at some numbers.

A barrel of oil in 1966 cost 2.75 grams in gold today you can buy a barrel of oil for just 1 gram. Check out the dollar purchasing power. In the same year a barrel cost \$3.10 at the time of writing \$40, a devaluation of 92%.

Countries selling oil, or indeed any commodity or manufactured good are beginning to realise they are falling into the category of those native Americans of yesteryear who sold Manhattan Island for a string of glass beads.

Where are we going?

As world economies mature this system will wither on the vine.

It is worth examining the Saudi position in some detail because it is a template at the moment for the geo-political position of other economies including China and Russia.

Saudi wealth is owned by their royal family, not the state.

The state (or royal) oil company, Aramco, is valued at $2 trillion give or take a billion. The Saudis are suffering from a fall in oil prices, it is, one need hardly remind folk a primitive society. To diversify their economy (assuming they can) they might consider selling 5% of their Aramco holdings, this would raise $100 billion, they have already raised a syndicated loan of $10 billion. A possible sale of $750 billion in U.S. Treasuries is on the cards.

Russia and China resent the petro dollar, not unreasonably. Asia and the Indian sub continent are marching towards a different system of settlement, anticipating abandoning American hegemony for ever.

The world is therefore neck deep in Yankee dollars which only carry perceived value in America. They must therefore repatriate eventually, a phenomenon which manifested itself post Vietnam.

The amounts are beyond the scope of human imagination.

It is in no one's interest to collapse U.S. treasuries least of all the Saudi royal family, Russian oligarchs, or Chinese Communist Party barons. But one thing is clear this bizarre fiscal phenomenon cannot continue ad infinitum.

World economies must start to ponder these problems before a neo con industrial military congressional solution manifests itself as the only identifiable option.

ACKNOWLEDGEMENTS

Compiling a short work is rather more difficult than a long one.

More a question of what to leave out, rather than what to put in.

The object of the work is to give interested lay folk from other professions and trades an idea of how their banking system works. I hope it is a little clearer now, I also hope it might have triggered an interest in some to take it further, to dig a bit deeper.

To this end, I am happy to thank very publicly those institutions which have produced superb essays over many years without which this short *aide memoire* would not have been possible.

The Institute of Economic Affairs, I have been a subscriber for over 30 years. The Von Mises Institute, at the cutting edge of this subject globally and essential membership for the Austrian School student. The Adam Smith Institute is also now beginning to rattle some cages. More power to their elbow.

I went across to my archive office to find some book titles which might help those embarking on deeper study and suggest the following, having been helped in focussing further on the questions, if not finding all the answers.

In no order of priority therefore:

Economics in One Lesson   Henry Hazlitt
John Maynard Keynes   Robert Skidelsky.
     MacMillan.

Liberty Through Gold	Prof. Hans Bocker. Johannes Muller
Inflation Tax	Peter Comley
The Austrian School	Jesus Huerta de Soto. Mises Inst.
Classical Economics	Murray Rothbard. Mises Inst.
America's Great Depression	Murray Rothbard. Mises Inst.
Economic Thought Before	
Adam Smith	Murray Rothbard. Mises Inst.
The Mystery of Banking	Murray Rothbard. Mises Inst.
Paper Money Collapse	Detler S Schlichter. John Wiley & Sons
The Tragedy of the Euro	Philip Bagus
History of Interest Rates	S. Homer & R. Sylla. Wiley Finance.
Human Action	Von Mises. Mises Inst.
Social Statics or Conditions	
Essential to Human Happiness	Herbert Spencer. John Chapman.
Pillars of Prosperity	Ron Paul. Mises Institute
The Bastiat Collection	Mises Institute
The Wages of Destruction	Adam Tooze. Penguin

The Death of the God Democracy Hans Hoppe.

These are just of the few which I found readable and informative.

But for those with limited time, most of us these days the IEA & Mises essays can bring you up to speed. They ate up my rail and air travel journeys for many years.

A personal thank you to Jeff Deist at the Mises Institute, Mark Littlewood at the IEA and Prof. Pat Barron always on hand for constructive advice also Gillian McLeod for her research and editing of graphics.